Essential Preparation for

UNDERGRADUATE MEDICINE & HEALTH SCIENCES ADMISSION TEST

Series One

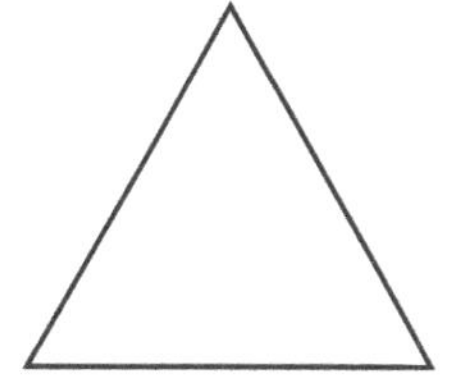

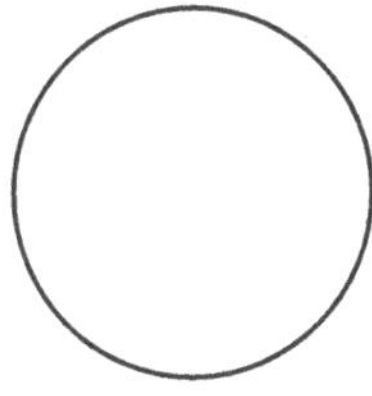

BOOK 2
UNDERSTANDING PEOPLE

Mohan Dhall

Five Senses Education Pty Ltd
2/195 Prospect Highway
Seven Hills 2147
New South Wales
Australia

First Published 2013

Dhall, Mohan
Book 2 - Understanding People

ISBN 978-1-74130-772-6

CONTENTS

UMAT Trial Examination

Total Test Time: 180 minutes

- **Section 1: 48 Questions (70 minutes)**
- **Section 2: 44 Questions (55 minutes)**
- **Section 3: 42 Questions (55 minutes)**

This book covers Section 2

Section 2 – Understanding People (55 minutes)

Number of questions: 44

Time allowed: 55 minutes

<u>Instructions to candidates</u>

This section assesses the ability to understand and reason about people. Questions are based on a scenario, dialogue or other text representing specific interpersonal situations. The questions will assess your ability to identify, understand, and, where necessary, infer the thoughts, feelings, behaviour and/or intentions of the people represented in the situations.

Questions 1 - 3

The following extract is taken from an account of an individual's experience of hip replacement surgery.

When I slipped I knew I had done some serious damage. At my age it is quite the talk – knees, hips, wrists and eyesight. I had heard about hip replacement surgery and never thought I would actually want it, but I had no choice. The surgeon was quite brusque though and clearly he was more interested in the actual procedure than me. Why should I matter? I am old and of little worth now except the pay cheque.

Unfortunately this was confirmed when I went for a post-operation appointment. The appointment lasted fifteen minutes and took place five days after surgery – earlier than the scheduled time. During that brief time I was with him the surgeon removed a bandage, pulling my skin painfully – I didn't even feel ready. A small bit of blood dripped and I felt nauseous. He then moved my leg, pressed the wound and admired his handiwork. The bruising was terrible, the swelling ugly and the manipulations felt strange. The surgeon's final response was, "smile, this looks great - all clear. I shall get the nurse to re-dress that and then it's off the physio with you." He then left in a hurry.

The nurse was much kinder. She said to me, "Poor darling, let's get you cleaned up." She then chatted gently to me and told me everything would be fine. That felt better. She offered to help me dress, but I am pretty independent and said no.

As I slowly dressed myself the receptionist came into the clinic and inquired as to whether I had brought payment.

Question 1

How did the patient perceive the manner of the surgeon post-operatively?

A) He was impatient and mercenary
B) He was self-centred and time pressured
C) He was reassuring but cold
D) He was an expert in the body but not in the emotions

Question 2

How did the patient feel while the surgeon removed the dressing?

A) Devalued
B) Brave
C) Unprepared
D) Embarrassed

Question 3

How did the patient's experience change when attended to by the nurse and the receptionist respectively?

A) Supported and understood, to objectified
B) Sympathised with and encouraged, to devalued
C) Normalised and included, to excluded
D) Intrinsically valued to superfluous

Questions 4 - 6

Elizabeth 'Betty' Robinson was born in 1911 in Riverdale, Illinois and went to school in a town called Harvey, two trains stops away. The train station at Riverdale was on a hilltop. One of Robinson's teachers was catching the train at Riverdale station one morning when he saw Robinson at the bottom of the hill. The train was about to depart as the guard was blowing his whistle. Upon hearing the whistle Robinson raced up the hill and bounded up the stairs, making the train with a second to spare. Her teacher raised his eyebrows. At the end of the day he timed Robinson running over 50 yards in a school corridor. Watching her run he thought that she should enter into competitions. Her teachers bought her spikes and entered her into races. In her second race Robinson equalled the world record of 100 metres in 12.0 seconds. Her third meeting was the qualifier for the 1928 Olympic games. At those games and as a seventeen-year-old, Robinson won the first ever women's athletics gold medal.

On a hot day in 1931, while preparing for the 1932 Olympic games Robinson was not allowed to train. It was so hot that Robinson asked her cousin, a pilot, to take her in his biplane in order that she could cool down in the open cockpit. The plane lost control at a height of 130 metres and crashed into the ground. Robinson's body was removed from the wreckage and driven to an undertaker by her rescuer. The undertaker said she was in a coma. Robinson remained in a coma for seven weeks. When she came out of the coma she was in a wheelchair for six months and she later found that the injuries she sustained stopped her from crouching for sprints. She gave up on running and concentrated on recuperation, which took two years. Robinson was told she would never walk without a cane and could never compete again. Three years later Robinson decided to try to jog. Shortly afterwards she rejoined her old athletics club and despite a stiff knee qualified for the 1936 Olympic games. There, as part of the US relay team she won a silver medal.

Question 4

What role does the Robinson's teacher play in her life?

A) Mentor
B) Tormentor
C) Chance factor
D) Guide

Question 5

How would the rescuer have felt when the undertaker said Robinson was alive, but unconscious?

A) Surprised and shocked
B) Shocked and embarrassed
C) Ashamed and hopeful
D) Shocked and relieved

Question 6

Why did Robinson rejoin her old club?

A) She needed the support of others who were training hard
B) She wanted to push herself to compete again
C) She wanted to show them that she was still capable
D) She wanted to thank them for all they had done for her

Questions 7 - 9

The following is a conversation between a father and his son.

Father: I know you and Carly are pretty close, but mate... mate... she seems pretty restrictive. I mean a man's a man. You gotta tell her what you want. The footy season's only short but she'll be with you forever.

Son: I reckon I should support her. Brandon's only three months old.

Father: Geez...you're like your mum. Brandon's sleeping – he'll be fine. Even if he wakes up, fat lot of good you can do mate. Besides, you'll just end up getting angry cos you're not at the footy. Better to be real mate.

Son: Dad! It's not that important.

Father: What happened to you mate? Become a wuss...?

Son: Dad! I just want to be with Carly. We need to buy some stuff for the house...

Father: Dammit! I thought I had a son, not two daughters. Next you'll be telling me she wants you to move to Queensland and you'll be watching the Bold and the Beautiful instead of watching the footy.

Son: I'm sorry Dad but I'm happy with the decision I have made.

Father: (sighs and leaves the house, banging the door and waking Brandon)

Question 7

What initiates the father's reaction to his son?

A) He is frustrated at his son's apparent weakness
B) He is angry because his son is controlled by Carly
C) He is disappointed that his son wants to stay at home
D) He is upset that his son is wasting time when the football is about to begin

Question 8

How would the son's response to his father be best characterised?

A) Apologetic and uncertain
B) Quiet but determined
C) Calm and contrite
D) Determined and respectful

Question 9

What is the father's stated view of relationships?

A) Men are in control and should not involve themselves in household matters
B) Parenting and housework is best left to women
C) Men should do traditionally male things such as play sport and watch sport
D) Women are too controlling and men should be strong when setting limits on what they are prepared to do

Questions 10 - 12

The following is an extract from an incident recalled by a young woman studying to be a psychologist when reflecting on her childhood.

I came home from school in Year Five following another fight with the girls. I was always the one being picked on. My mother said to me, "Just listen to me. They are not as good as you. They don't like you being so smart and they hate it when you are right. Don't worry about them. I was just like you and look at how many friends I have now..."

Her words washed over me and after a while she was as far away as they were – just shadows in the doorway. The evening came and went and I never knew what would happen next. At school I was on the ceiling or outside the window or somewhere else looking in. It went like that throughout the next four years. "How was school?" and before I could finish my reply the advice tumbling out again like an uncontrollable landslide. Then one day I didn't speak. I smiled. She paused. And after that my voice came back and I landed.

Question 10

What does the passage suggest about the mother's capacity to help solve her daughter's problems?

A) She is upset about the girls fighting with her daughter and wants her daughter to cope through hope
B) She is well-meaning but limited in her ability to resolve conflict
C) She is capable of helping her daughter but the daughter has to comply
D) She is confident and righteous in her approach to problem-solving

Question 11

Which one of the following best describes how the daughter is feeling?

A) Lost and alone
B) Afraid and isolated
C) Watchful and alert
D) Apprehensive and isolated

Question 12

Which of the following would have been most helpful in the first instance to the girl when she was in Year Five?

A) Her mother saying 'You feel upset and alone. I know Sweetheart...'
B) Her mother phoning the other parents and telling them about the bullying
C) Allowing the daughter to handle the other girls without any advice whatsoever
D) Advising the girl to ignore the bullies and say nothing to anyone

Questions 13 - 16

In the following passage a man recounts his experience of an accident, the surgery and post-operative experience.

The music was on loud and the car was moving very fast. The driver, my friend, was talking to me as we sped along the highway. Although he was younger than me he already has his license. I had just left school. He said to me, I can drive on the verge. I come from the bush and we know how to handle cars on gravel." He then placed the front and back left-hand wheels on the gravel while two remained on the bitumen. We travelled like that for about 200 metres, feeling the bumpiness of the gravel to our left. He then moved the car totally onto the gravel and immediately lost control. I shut my eyes. The car leapt across the road leaving angry black lines across the lanes and then bounced through some scrub and crashed sideways into a huge tree truck. The collision was so violent that the car then spun around two hundred and seventy degrees.

When I opened my eyes my seat was raised and angled over the gear stick. In front of my forehead the car was crushed to within a centimetre of my hairline. I pushed my friend out. I had to unbuckle his seatbelt. He sat there staring ahead in silence. I dragged myself out with my arms and tried to stand but my right leg buckled. I tried to stand with my left leg and hopped to the side of the dark road thinking if I get home then I could tell my parents I fell down the back stairs. They were away. They were always away. As luck would have it, the first car I stopped had a two-way radio and quickly called for help. The ambulance took me to the emergency ward. My leg was so swollen my jeans had to be cut off me, from ankle to hip. The next day I had the surgery.

The ward I was allocated to was shared by three other men; two old and one a few years older than me. He had been in a motorbike accident and had a metal pin through his lower shinbone to pull his leg downwards from his hip and correct the alignment and leg length. He could not leave his bed and the smell of his morning ablutions and the sound of his singing to mask the sounds will remain with me forever. It was hardly what I could have imagined. The older men complained incessantly.

During recovery I needed a catheter* put in and it was painful and uncomfortable, especially when removed. I needed to learn to urinate again without it. I had to relax and push simultaneously and visions of the catheter being reacquainted helped me find that balance. The doctors came and checked my progress but I never knew their names and they always moved quickly. The days were long and the sky outside seemed large. After five days my head felt itchy and I noticed I had glass fragments in my scalp. I had to scratch to remove one, and then a nurse came with tweezers and took out the rest. How did we miss that? Later I got a wheelchair and learnt to do wheelies down the hallway – but mostly being out of the ward for a while was freedom.

*A catheter is a tube placed into the urethra to drain away urine

Question 13

"Although he was younger than me he already had his license" (lines 2 and 3). This suggests that the author feels

A) Aggrieved
B) Resentful
C) Envious
D) Rueful

Question 14

The author's relationship with his parents is best described as

A) Close and trusting
B) Distant and unsupportive
C) Fearful and tense
D) Respectful and cold

Question 15

What was the author's experience of the ward?

A) He enjoyed the company of others because it would have been too quiet otherwise
B) He became frustrated by the lack of personal care and attention
C) He learnt that others have bigger struggles and came to accept the situation
D) He struggled to accept the feeling of restriction and the loss of control

Question 16

"How did we miss that?" (Lines 36 and 37). The author at this point is most likely to feel

A) Exasperated
B) Disbelieving
C) Ignored
D) Abandoned

Questions 17 - 21

The following extract is taken from a letter written by a son to his mother. The son had just left the hospital where his father is very close to death. The mother and father separated amicably when the son was two-years-old and he grew up with his father.

Dear Mother,

"See...shells! See...shells! Seashells! And if you listen closely when we are at home the sound of today will still be in there..." That's my earliest memory of Dad. I just came back and I keep having images of those days at the beach. Remember the hermit crabs we once had? One day I picked up a shell at the beach but it felt too light. The crab had gone in search of another home. Dad called out, "Search for the naked crab!" and we ran all over laughing and looking. Then I saw he had drawn a 'naked' hermit crab in the sand close to the water with its front legs covering its 'doodle'. "Found it!" he shouted, but as I ran to look closer the water washed over it and when it retreated the crab was gone. "Modesty", said Dad. "That's my kind of hermit".

Dad looked like the shell today. His skin was pale and grey simultaneously. His eyes oozed stuff and the beach was flat. The fishermen's buckets were empty and an overcast sky hung still over us. The water looked larger and stiller than ever and I felt smaller than a sand particle, ready to be washed away.

On the way home I cried until I couldn't cry anymore. As I write this, an empty shell is still on my desk. I picked it up to listen and heard the sound of the sea and the sound of silence together and I wanted to pick one sound but they were blended too smoothly.

Where has he gone?

Love always, Your Sun (behind a cloud today)

Question 17

How does the author feel after visiting his father in hospital?

A) Broken and bereft
B) Sad and lonely
C) Sorrowful and reflective
D) Angry and distressed

Question 18

Why does the author repeat the word 'still' in the second and third paragraphs?

A) Stillness keeps things the same and unchanged
B) Stillness does not allow distractions to take a moment away
C) Still means there will be more time before his father dies
D) Time feels still when memories and the present mix

Question 19

What is the significance of the statement, "search for the naked crab!" (Lines 6 and 7)?

A) It is the author's earliest memory when he thinks back
B) The author is searching for the father he remembers
C) Death is mysterious and unknown
D) The author is searching for answers

Question 20

What does the hermit crab represent?

A) Transition
B) Growth
C) Change
D) Loss

Question 21

Which word would best describe how the mother would feel after reading this letter?

A) Protective
B) Bereft
C) Lonely
D) Ambivalent

Questions 22 - 25

The following is a recount of a conversation between a mother and a daughter on the subject of vaccination and immunisation. The daughter is Jennifer and the mother is Denise.

"So, it's been a few weeks now and you've had time to re-consider the 'no vaccination' rubbish", Denise said as she started the conversation. "Your father is a doctor so you really ought to know better than question those who know. I mean, really."

"Oh, hi Mum. Great. We are well and the baby is fine. Thanks for asking. How's Dad?"

"Don't be silly Darling and stop avoiding the issue. When shall I take you and the baby to the clinic for the first shots? I can do it this morning if you are too scared to do it yourself."

"Mum! We are not afraid. We just need more time to think about whether it is necessary or..."

"Jennifer. Darling. Necessary...? I think that silly boy-husband of yours has made you more crazy than you were without him. Don't tell me he is still on about that homeopathic mumbo jumbo and that vaccination and immunisation are two different things. I call it psychopathic trollop. Now, be grown up and let's get the baby what it needs to be strong and healthy."

"Stop Mum! Have you finished? I didn't say no. We just want to investigate whether SIDS*, allergies and anaphylaxis, cancers and side effects are related to vaccination..."

"This is just meaningless Darling. What an insult to your father and me. Are you telling me we gave you cancer-inducing injections as a child? What nonsense! Listen to me. You always were a bit silly when it came to mature decisions. Your choice of husband shows that. I'm coming over now and we'll sort this out properly."

*Sudden Infant Death Syndrome

Question 22

How would Jennifer view her mother's offer of support?

A) Generous and supportive
B) Condescending and helpful
C) Decisive and intrusive
D) Controlling and patronising

Question 23

When Jennifer says, "Have you finished?" her intention is to

A) Set limits around her mother
B) Find her voice again
C) Have her turn in the conversation
D) Justify herself to her mother

Question 24

The conversation reveals that Denise thinks Jennifer's husband is

A) Considerate
B) Unpredictable
C) Immature
D) Dim witted

Question 25

Jennifer's approach to the situation shows that she is

A) Strong and determined
B) Aligned with her husband
C) Independent and feisty
D) Passive and weak

Questions 26 - 29

This is an extract from an interview with the mother of a child with a profound disability.

I so looked forward to having my first child. I loved looking after my half-brother and half-sister when they were growing up and I always knew I would be very involved mother. I laboured for over 24-hours and then had to have an emergency caesarean when the heart monitor recorded foetal distress. Anyway when Howard was born it was immediately obvious something was wrong. He didn't make a sound and the operating theatre fell silent. In the next few days I was separated from him and he was in the ICU* to monitor the fits he was having. I asked the doctors what they did to my son but they never replied. After we went home it was to a silent house. I have tried everything with Howard – mainstream medicine, alternative therapies, massage, chiropractic remedies, acupuncture... even emerging therapies. Nothing works. Howard is blind. He cannot really move on his own. He has no muscle tone and cannot communicate except with grunts and yelps. He must be carried everywhere. He cannot swallow and must be fed by hand.

Howard is now 18-years-old. When he was four I decided to have another baby. My mind screamed no, but I went ahead regardless. Thankfully, Howard's sister was born in hospital without incident and she is fine. After that I became bolder and tried for a third baby, but after I miscarried four times I knew that was it. I had always wanted five children.

Disability services in Australia are so woeful. I could not get proper care for Howard while I worked. If he had fewer disabilities he would have been fine. As a carer I faced discrimination trying to get flexible working hours and as an advocate for my son came up against barrier after barrier. It's been really hard and I have learnt a lot. I never expected the life I have had, but you adjust and do the best you can. One day Howard will walk and when he does it will show the world what love can do. Meantime his rights matter as much as those of a full-functioning child.

*Intensive Care Unit

Question 26

The mother's view of the medical authorities is that they are

A) reckless and need to be held to account
B) careful and considerate
C) ambivalent and there to be used as required
D) useless and should be mistrusted

Question 27

"My mind screamed no, but I went ahead regardless" (Second paragraph). Here the woman reveals that she felt

A) Uncertain
B) Petrified
C) Vulnerable
D) Brave

Question 28

What is the woman's experience of disability services?

A) They focus on children with low-level disabilities
B) They are unable to cope with too many demands
C) They cannot handle children with more than one disability
D) They are underfunded

Question 29

The statement, "One day Howard will walk and when he does it will show the world what love can do" suggests that the woman

A) Believes she is the only one who loves and knows Howard
B) Struggles to accept her son's disabilities
C) Feels the world is against her but she will prove them wrong
D) Still carries hope about the prospect of her son recovering

Questions 30 - 33

This is an account of a bushfire that occurred last summer. The couple talking here lost their home and their two pet dogs.

Her: "The fire came up the rise quickly. We had heard the warning and fire danger bulletins all week but when it became real we were still not prepared. The insects and birds came ahead of the smoke. I saw all these black beetles flying over me and the birds were silent and determined as they flew past. The smell went deep into me..."

Him: "The RFS* came up the road and said, 'GO!' so we grabbed a couple of things. As I opened the door the missus said to me 'get the dogs' but as I turned back to the house the embers burnt holes in my shirt and the heat and smoke made me turn back... I opened the car door and embers started to burn the seats so we jumped inside and as I slammed the door shut I saw the helicopter just over the house...Me eyelashes were gone and me eyes were stingin'..."

Her: "We drove down the road beating the embers out. I burnt my hand and the back seat got full of holes. It was so hard to drive through the smoke and we hit a couple of parked cars as we went. We were the last to leave..."

Him: "Next morning we were allowed to return. We thought it would be bad, but nothin' prepares you for what we saw. My missus started cryin' as we got to our house. All night she worried about the dogs and when we got to where the house shoulda been there were only ashes and some smoke... we got out of the car and the ground was hot and everything was quiet. Much quieter than I had ever heard. Then I heard a tree falling in the area behind our burnt out block. The cracking of the tree, the smoke and the burnt land.... My God!"

Her: "I knew straight away we'd lost everything. I couldn't speak. It wasn't real. Everything I owned and everything I knew was gone. I could see the whole neighbourhood because there were no trees or houses. We later heard that Les died trying to save his house. We lost the house but what mattered to me more was Jessie and Freddie. Poor things... what a way to die. I believe dogs have feelings and I hate to imagine what they might have felt as the fire closed in."

*Rural Fire Service

Question 30

The couple could best be described as

A) Well prepared and ready
B) Confused and disorientated
C) Taken by surprise
D) Responsive to a changing situation

Question 31

As the couple left their house they would have felt

A) Secure knowing that the RFS would save their property and dogs
B) Scared and uncertain about themselves and their house and dogs
C) Determined not to live in a fire-prone area again
D) Concerned about when they could return to check on everything

Question 32

Upon returning the woman felt

A) Numb
B) Disorientated
C) Scared
D) Lost

Question 33

Why does the woman 'hate to imagine what they felt as the fire closed in'?

A) She feels guilty that she could not protect her dogs
B) She feels like they must have tried to escape on their own
C) She feels disappointed that the dogs died
D) She feels upset that they are gone forever

Questions 34 - 37

The following account comes from a discussion between three people: Marcus a doctor, a senior ministerial health advisor called Stan and a man with uncurable cancer, Jake.

Jake: Sure I smoke dope. I need it to handle the pain. I have a medical prescription for opiate-based pain relief that I got while travelling overseas. When I got back the authorities asked me to take a drug test. I said no. After that they stopped my treatment. The rule is that if they find any illegal drugs in your system they will not give you any pain treatment. That is unfair. I've been getting this pain treatment for years, but overseas - not here.

Stan: Marijuana is a controlled substance and its sale and manufacture are prohibited by the *Drug Misuse and Trafficking Act*. Every sale of marijuana is illegal and is treated as trafficking. The government could thus arrest every person who sells marijuana regardless of the reason for the sale.

Marcus: Pain relief is a significant aspect of patient management. Opiate-based relief comes in several forms and has been found to be effective in providing comfort to those with terminal illnesses.

Stan: But how terminal is terminal? Jake says he's been getting treatment for years...

Jake: Are you serious? The big pharmaceutical companies that have you on their payroll do not want to lose control of the market. A government-controlled system of marijuana sales to those who need it would be appropriate. We are not talking here about heavy drugs - just something to help me manage the cancer pain.

Marcus: As far as I am aware no-one ever overdosed on marijuana. Alcohol and hard drugs are different. Nevertheless, questions remain about the safety of marijuana use on persons vulnerable to schizophrenia. More research needs to be done.

Stan: Why change a system that is already working? We have palliative care and we have huge investment in pain management and there is a wide-range of pain relief medications. Just because it might work doesn't mean it's the best solution. A bomb can be used to put out a fire, but so can water.

Question 34

In this conversation Jake is feeling

A) Determined and certain
B) Confused and judged
C) Victimised and angry
D) Misrepresented and upset

Question 35

The doctor's position on the use of marijuana as evidenced by the conversation is one of

A) Optimism
B) Openness
C) Skepticism
D) Conviction

Question 36

Stan could best be described as

A) Pragmatic
B) Protective
C) Stable
D) Conservative

Question 37

"But how terminal is terminal?" In his response to Stan's comment, Jake tries to

A) Regain equality in the discussion by exposing Stan
B) Hurt Stan because he feels hurt by Stan
C) Widen the discussion so that it is more inclusive of different perspectives
D) Support his opening statement

Questions 38 - 41

In the following extract a man relays his experience of mental illness having spent time with his schizophrenic brother

I am walking with my brother on the streets of Sheffield. He has been cold and the winter is bitter. I struggle to keep up with him. We are heading to the music store and he wants to spend the pension money he just received. He has always spent money like pouring water out of a jug. As we get closer to the shopping centre the number of people about increases. Soon we are walking through crowds. Suddenly, and without warning, my brother kicks a lady in the stomach. I am startled and so is she. I pull my brother aside as he says, "She tried to get me, she's evil..."

We are asleep in his halfway house and I wake to check on him. He is quivering and his body is shaky. I watch him in the half-light. He is fitful in his sleep and I am afraid for him. I wonder where he is in his sleep and I wonder where he is when he is awake. In the morning I comment on his shaking. He tells me not to worry – the medication has that effect and keeps the visions at bay. And besides, at least then he is drug free.

Another time I am talking to him and I notice a scar in his hairline. I ask him what happened. He replies, "Oh can you see that?" which surprises me. I say, "What happened?" He pauses, pushes his hair over the scar and replies, "When they jailed me for shoplifting I was put into a cell with a very large man. I asked him what he was in for. He told me it was murder and I laughed thinking he was joking. He then beat me unconscious and the guards took their sweet time before they helped me..."

I am talking to the Supreme Court judge. I ask her if she could change one thing what it would be. She says criminal justice sometimes is not just. That thirty percent of the people she sends to jail have a mental illness. She says, "I wish I could send them for treatment but we do not have the health care facilities to look after them...". This reminds me of the time my brother told me he would shoplift in order to get a meal in the prison cell. A meal, and a scar for grace.

My brother grows a heavy beard. He shaves his head. Gets a tattoo of an eagle across his back. Sends me a photo of himself shirtless and smoking. Tells me how much he hates being medicated – that drugs are better and he knows how to score. Tells me he is Bodi Satva come to save the world. That he cannot wear leather because animals feel pain too. Tells me that all of life is a circle and that all authorities oppress people. Later he escapes from supervised care and jumps from a bridge breaking both ankles. Now he hobbles and has physical pain as well as visions.

Question 38

In this sentence, 'I wonder where he is in his sleep and I wonder where he is when he is awake.' what is the author hoping to convey?

A) That he does not know his brother
B) That the effects of schizophrenia cannot be understood by anyone
C) That sleeping and waking are the same for schizophrenic sufferers
D) That he wants to reach his brother

Question 39

When his brother says, "Oh can you see that?" why is the author surprised?

A) He did not think his brother would be self-conscious
B) He thinks his brother feels guilty for being hit
C) He realises there is a story behind the scar
D) He senses that his brother has forgotten an incident he does not want to recall

Question 40

How does the Supreme Court judge feel when she passes jail sentences on those she thinks need medical care?

A) Guilty
B) Regretful
C) Powerless
D) Disappointed

Question 41

The purpose of the author's last paragraph is to

A) Keep a diary of what his brother said and did
B) Give the reader an insight into the behaviour of schizophrenics
C) Try and make sense of a rapidly changing situation involving a loved one
D) To track the changes so that others know what to do when faced with a similar situation

Questions 42 - 44

Three women are discussing the effects of obesity on their lives. A transcript of their conversation is detailed below.

Jane: The name 'FATTS' is appropriate for our group because it stands for 'Fat Adults Trying To Slim'. It is important that we accept ourselves and take ownership for what we are trying to achieve.

Codi: You know...about 25% of Australians are obese. We are a minority group. But actually we are in the majority by weight! Haha... Why not call ourselves the 'Twenty-five Percenters'...?

Jess: I'd prefer that to FATTS. Gosh I'm having trouble looking at myself, and I hate the supermarket stares. Why would I demean myself by labelling myself FATT? We should call ourselves 'SLIM' - the Support group for Ladies IMagining... a future.

Jane: Seriously Jess? Really? You are in denial. We should start with where we are at.

Jess: No...we should focus on where we want to be. I'm tired of being fat. I am tired of being slow, of struggling into my car, of being stared at when I shop...

Codi: So we are real. It's hard. One day I was normal and then bang! I was married with teenage kids, driving all over town, working long hours and suddenly I wonder where my body went. And, where my life went.

Question 42

How does Jane feel about Jess's opening statement?

A) Misunderstood
B) Rejected
C) Dejected
D) Frustrated

Question 43

How does Jess feel when she is shopping?

A) Judged
B) Worthless
C) Unsupported
D) Desperate

Question 44

What does Codi mean when she says "and suddenly I wonder where my body went" ?

A) She has trouble accepting her life
B) Things she needs to do overwhelm her
C) Things happened at a pace she cannot understand
D) She wants to be young again

ANSWERS

Summary & Worked Solutions
Multiple Choice Answer Sheet

Summary of Answers

Question 1	B	Question 12	A	Question 23	A	Question 34	C
Question 2	C	Question 13	C	Question 24	C	Question 35	B
Question 3	A	Question 14	B	Question 25	B	Question 36	D
Question 4	C	Question 15	D	Question 26	C	Question 37	B
Question 5	D	Question 16	A	Question 27	B	Question 38	D
Question 6	B	Question 17	C	Question 28	A	Question 39	A
Question 7	C	Question 18	D	Question 29	D	Question 40	C
Question 8	D	Question 19	B	Question 30	C	Question 41	C
Question 9	B	Question 20	A	Question 31	B	Question 42	D
Question 10	B	Question 21	A	Question 32	A	Question 43	A
Question 11	D	Question 22	D	Question 33	A	Question 44	C

Answers with fully worked solutions

Question 1

B

There is no evidence that the surgeon was mercenary, but there is plenty of evidence that the patient perceives the surgeon as self-centred ('more interested in the actual procedure than me' and 'admired his handiwork'). The surgeon is also busy (he was 'brusque' and 'left in a hurry') thus B is the correct response.

Question 2

C

The patient says "I didn't even feel ready" so clearly she feels unprepared for the removal of the dressing. There is nothing to indicate the patient feels devalued in this encounter with the surgeon.

Question 3

A

The choice here is really between A and B. The nurse was empathetic rather than sympathetic and thus supported and understood is a more accurate account of the experience from the patient's perspective. The receptionist asking for money did not devalue the patient but does objectify her to a client who has to pay the money rather than as a person who must be feeling in need of support following major surgery. Thus A is correct.

Question 4

C

A mentor tends to have an on-going role in a person's life but the teacher had more of a 'discovery role' and with other teachers supported Robinson to buy spikes and enter competitions. None of the teachers seems to be an expert in sprinting or manage her, thus C is the best response. A chance factor is an unexpected occurrence that can change a person's life for the better.

Question 5

D

The rescuer thought that Robinson had died even though she was in a coma. Thus once the undertaker noted that she was alive the rescuer would have been shocked rather than surprised. Hence A can be omitted. The rescuer is unlikely to have felt ashamed at mistaking Robinson for being dead, though it is possible. C can also therefore be omitted. Since the rescuer would also not have likely felt embarrassed at making a mistake when a person thought dead is alive B can also be omitted. It is most likely that the shock of realising that Robinson is alive would be followed by relief, hence D is correct.

Question 6

B

Robinson would most likely have wondered how far she could push herself given that jogging was more than she was told was possible. Robinson jogged and then 'shortly after' rejoined her old athletics club. She was already committed and thus A is not likely. There is nothing to indicate that Robinson ever needed to prove herself to others hence C can be discounted. There is also no evidence that her old club supported her recovery hence D is not correct.

Question 7

C

The father really wants his son to join him but the son's priority is on his own family. Thus he is not weak and A can be eliminated. Nor does Carly control the son as the son is making his own decisions: 'I reckon I should support her' and 'I just want to be with Carly'. Hence B is incorrect. D can also be discounted as there is no evidence of the son wasting time.

What is clear is that the father wants the son to come to the football with him but the son has opted to stay as home and prioritise things of greater importance to him. Hence C is correct.

Question 8

D

The son says 'sorry' but his tone is not apologetic. Rather the son is strong, certain and determined. This is evidenced by how he repeatedly affirms what he wants to do. However he is also respectful and thus D is correct.

Question 9

B

The father has a particularly old fashioned view of male-female relationships, disparaging the son's decision to support his partner by calling him a 'wuss'. He also accuses his son of being a 'daughter' because he wants to buy things for the house. The attitude coming through these statements from the father is that parenting and housework is left to women.

Whilst the father does suggest men should be stronger it is not his stated view that men should not be involved in household matters. Hence A is incorrect. Nowhere does the father suggest that his son or men generally should *play* sport thus C is incorrect. The father does not generalise 'control' to all women thus D is incorrect.

Question 10

B

The mother does not express hopefulness but is rather quite active and directive in her advice to her daughter. Thus A is not correct. Whilst the mother says 'just listen to me' there is no evidence that her advice would actually or does actually make any difference. Thus C is not correct. The frequency of the mother's advice and the haste with which it is delivered suggests that the mother is not confident at all with how to manage, though she is quite self-righteous. This eliminates D.

What is clear is that the mother is well meaning and trying to assist her daughter but does not have the skill or ability to do so – hence B is correct.

Question 11

D

The daughter is alone or isolated as she feels on the 'outside...looking in'. Thus C with the word 'alert' is incorrect. There is no evidence that the daughter is afraid hence B can be eliminated as well, This leaves A and D. The girl does not suggest she was lost as she always knew where she was: 'on the ceiling', 'outside the window or somewhere else looking in'. Hence A is not right. The daughter does say "I never knew what would happen next' – consistent with a feeling of apprehension.

Hence D is correct.

Question 12

A

If the mother had called all of the other parents then it could have been a gross over reaction and could lead to a rupture of the friendships forever. Thus B is inappropriate. If the mother left her daughter to handle the situation on her own she would have felt abandoned thus C is not helpful and should be discounted. Ignoring bullies is a passive approach and advising the daughter to say nothing is akin to silencing her, which could be very destructive. Thus D is inappropriate.

Empathy is always likely to be helpful as it is affirming and understanding. Hence A is an approach likely to be most helpful and is the correct response.

Question 13

C

Aggrieved is too strong a term and the passing thought does not suggest resentment towards his friend. It is likely he feels envious of his younger friend's independence. Thus C is correct. Rueful means sorrowful or regretful and is not the appropriate feeling for this situation hence D is not correct.

Question 14

B

The author says, 'They were away. They were always away', shortly after having thought about ways of lying to his parents. This suggests low levels of trust and that his parents were physically and emotionally distant. Hence A can be discounted. They do not appear elsewhere in the recount despite the son having surgery and spending a long time in hospital. This suggests that his parents are unsupportive.

There is no evidence of respect or tension hence C and D can be discounted as well.

Question 15

D

The author certainly did not enjoy the others in the ward. His description indicates that it was uncomfortable and he did not like the others. Thus A is not correct. The author does not complain of a lack of personal care or attention, thus B is not correct. Whilst there is a reference to another patient recovering from serious surgery there is no evidence of the struggles faced by other patients leading to some personal insight about acceptance, hence C is not correct.

The author values his freedom when he gets a wheelchair and seems to feel quite bored "the days were long and the sky outside seemed large". Thus D is correct.

Question 16

A

The fact that the glass was missed and that this is discovered by the author rather than the medical staff five days into his recovery, would lead to a feeling of exasperation. That is, he would be frustrated in the context of feeling restricted and uncomfortable.

Question 17

C

Bereft is a feeling associated with loss and grief. "Sad" is too non-specific a feeling, thus B is not correct. There is no evidence of any anger or distress thus D is incorrect.

The author is clearly feeling sorrowful and reflecting on past memories, thus C is correct.

Question 18

D

The word 'still' appears three times: "The fishermen's buckets were empty and an overcast sky hung <u>still</u> over us", "The water looked larger and <u>still</u>er than ever..." and "...an empty shell is <u>still</u> on my desk". Each of these references takes the reader to a time in the life of the author when the author and his father were together. Thus the times past, as remembered and the present mix and time stands still.

Question 19

B

The statement "search for the naked crab!" is a metaphor used in this context by the author to represent vulnerability and transition. The author is recalling some connecting times with his father, but those times are never to be repeated as his father is dying. Thus the symbolism and significance of the statement is that the author is searching for something not changing and not vulnerable, that he has known in the past - the father her remembers.

Question 20

A

The hermit crab represents the move from one phase in life to another - outgrowing one shell and leaving it empty and moving to a new home. This is much more than change. It is transition from one thing to another with no return.

Whilst the crab is moving from a smaller shell to a larger one the symbolism is not one of growth. This is because the 'transition' is from life to death. The crab is also not symbolic of loss – although the (empty) shell may well be.

Question 21

A

The answer to this must lie in the context of the mother's relationship with her son (Sun') whom evidently she is close to. Thus we cannot assume she would be lonely and C must be discounted. 'Sad' is too simplistic – sad about what in particular? She may feel ambivalent because the man who fathered her son is dying, but they are separate. This may the case but it also may not be – it is not certain.

One thing is certain. The son is close enough with his mother to be very open and vulnerable. It is highly likely that a mother reading this account would feel very protective of her son and try to shield him from the pain and the sorrow he is going through. Thus A is correct.

Question 22

D

Jennifer's mother is quite pushy and demanding and full of disparaging comments about both her and her husband. Thus Jennifer would not see the offer as generous or supportive, hence A can be ruled out. Whilst the mother is condescending and clearly believes that she knows what it best, this is far from helpful for Jennifer. Hence B can also be ruled out. Whilst the behaviour of the mother appears to be decisive from Jennifer's perspective that is not important. The more prevalent feeling is one of control and of Jennifer's mother being condescending or patronising. Hence D is correct.

Question 23

A

Jennifer appears throughout the conversation to have strength and self-assurance. Thus, 'finding her voice' is not an issue. Moreover, Jennifer is able to contribute regularly in the conversation and thus would not be 'waiting her turn'. Whilst Jennifer does explain her position after saying "Have you finished? Mum, I didn't say no" her primary intention would be to set limits around her mother by restricting her and taking back power. The later justification only adds to setting those boundaries. In all likelihood this conversation has been had several times in the past 'it has been a few weeks now' and the mother will already have heard Jennifer's side of the situation. Thus A is correct, not D.

Question 24

C

The mother makes a reference to Jennifer's husband as a 'boy-husband'. Later she asks her daughter to 'grow up'. Clearly, Denise, the mother, has a view that Jennifer's husband is immature.

Question 25

B

There is nothing to indicate that Jennifer is weak or immature, thus D can be discounted from consideration. Jennifer seems courteous throughout, despite setting limits around her mother's control and subtle aggression. Hence she cannot be called 'feisty' (fiery), so C is not correct. Both A and B are possible so the text must be read carefully. On four occasions Jennifer uses the term 'we' in reference to her husband and herself. She is clearly aligned with her husband. Jennifer also appears to be open – 'I didn't say no' and 'we just need more time' - thus whilst she sounds determined it is arguable that she is also strong. The better answer is B.

Question 26

C

The statement 'I asked the doctors what they did to my son but they never replied' can be read as the doctors needing to being held to account or that the doctors were too busy doing what they had to do to support Howard that they could not reply. Further, her second baby was born in hospital without complications, thus she was not adverse to using hospitals and doctors. Hence A can be ruled out as can D. There is no suggestion that there is particular care or consideration accorded to the mother, thus B can be eliminated. C is the only answer consistent with the mother's statements.

Question 27

B

Petrified technically means frozen or numb with fear. This betrays very deep emotion and in the context of this situation, angst at possible loss. All of the other words are relevant feelings for the mother to have but none carries the weight or portrays the depth of emotion evoked by the situation facing the mother. Thus B is correct.

Question 28

A

The text needs to be read very carefully here. The woman states that if her son 'had fewer disabilities' he would have been fine. This suggests that disability services tend to focus on children with low-level disabilities, rather than an inability to cope with too many demands. Moreover it cannot be read into the text that disability services cannot handle children with more than one disability hence C can be dismissed. As there is no reference to funding (direct or implied) D cannot be correct

Hence A is the best response.

Question 29

D

There is nothing in the text to suggest that the mother does not accept her son's disabilities, hence B can be discounted. She does not also express any 'siege' mentality of the world being against her, despite her struggles. Thus, C is incorrect. Whilst the mother probably knows her son best this is not the correct interpretation of the statement hence C can be ruled out.

The mother has tried numerous and varied remedies and interventions and still carries hope that her son will improve. Thus, D is correct.

Question 30

C

The woman says in her opening statement that they were 'still not prepared'. This is indicative of feeling surprise as they were not fully ready. Thus C is correct.

Question 31

B

As the couple left their house they would have been thinking and feeling many things, but none of them would be certain, hence A can be ruled out. They also would have been in the immediacy of the moment, rather than thinking ahead to when they could return thus D can also be ruled out. The thought about living in a fire-prone area may have crossed the mind, but far more concerning would be whether they would make it out and whether the house and dogs would be safe. Thus, B is correct.

Question 32

A

Upon returning the woman started crying and she herself recounts that she "...couldn't speak" and that "It wasn't real". These are messages consistent with shock, thus 'numb' or A is the best response.

Question 33

A

The woman here is making a reference to her dogs. The woman cannot know whether or not the dogs tried to escape, hence B is incorrect. The woman feels deeply distressed that the dogs have died, thus C "disappointed" does not convey anywhere near the depth of feeling experienced. Moreover, "upset" also does not convey the depth of experience. A loving owner having left her dogs would feel guilty that she could not protect her dogs from what must have been a horrible death. Thus A is correct.

Question 34

C

Whilst Jake may be determined and certain that is not the feeling that predominates. He does not come across as confused – Jake can articulate his thoughts cogently. Though he may feel unfairly judged, B is not correct. There is nothing to indicate that Jake has been misrepresented, though he would be upset. Hence D is not correct.

Jake's opening statement indicates that he is feeling victimised: "that is unfair". Moreover, he feels like he should not need to justify his decision: "we are not talking heavy drugs here – just something to help me manage the cancer pain".

Question 35

B

The doctor does not express optimism or pessimism. Nor does he engage in any conversation where skepticism is uncovered. However, the doctor is neither convinced of the need for marijuana nor adverse to more research. Thus he would be best described as 'open' and B is correct.

Question 36

D

Stan does not indicate that he is protective. He has a factual approach that supports a position already taken by the government and that supports no change to that arrangement. Hence 'stable' and protective are not appropriate terms to describe him. Pragmatic means practical and based on facts and evidence. The term could support a push in favour of change or in favour of no change. Hence this term cannot be applied to this situation in the context of the brief conversation. Stan is certainly conservative "why change a system that is already working?"

Question 37

B

There is nothing about Jake's response that indicates that he is supporting his own opening statement. Nor does he aim specifically to widen the discussion in order to allow for multiple perspectives. Hence C and D are not correct. It is more likely that he wants to say something that will hurt Stan through exposing his position, or rather the government's position. In this way B is a better answer than A.

Question 38

D

The author is not asserting that he does not know is brother in this statement, though the last paragraph seems to allude to this. Hence A is not correct. The statement is not a general one applicable to all people suffering from schizophrenia, but rather a reflective statement made in response to his brother's situation. It is also not a general statement made in regards to the state of sleeping and waking for all sufferers, hence B and C are incorrect.

In this sentence the author is saying that his brother is as far away in his sleep as he is to him when he is awake – at both times unreachable. Hence D is correct.

Question 39

A

It is unlikely a person would feel guilty for being struck thus B is not correct. Since it is likely that every scar would have a story then it would hardly be the source of surprise, hence C is not correct. The brother says "Oh can you see that?" not "Oh I forgot that". There is nothing to indicate it is forgotten hence D is not correct.

There does not seem much in the behaviour of the schizophrenic brother that suggests he reflects on what others think of him. Hence the author is surprised at the statement and the attempt to cover the scar with his hair.

Question 40

C

The judge is in a situation over which they have no control. This does not make her feel guilty as her strongest emotion. There may be some regret and some disappointment at the system but the strongest and most pervasive feeling is one of powerlessness as there are not the mental health facilities available for suffers of schizophrenia to obtain appropriate care and keep them out of the criminal justice system.

Question 41

C

The author is not using the situation in order to keep a personal diary thus A is not correct. The situation involving his brother may or may not be similar to the situation faced by others but the author does not appear to be doing anything other than trying to make sense of his brother's deteriorating situation in order to make sense of what is occurring - hence C is correct.

It may be the case that in his recount other carers may feel supported but this does not appear to be the intention of the author.

Question 42

D

Jane says, "Seriously Jess? Really? You are in denial..." This indicates that Jane feels as though Jess is focusing on something that is not important and this makes her irritated. Hence dejected, rejected and misunderstood are not correct terms that describe how Jane feels.

Question 43

A

When people stare at Jess she would feel like others are evaluating her and being silently critical. Thus she would feel judged. Feelings of worthlessness may well arise from this but the primary feeling would be one of judgement.

Question 44

C

Codi does not indicate that she has any trouble accepting her life or that she feels any regret. Thus A and D are not correct. Nor does Codi indicate that she is overwhelmed by what she needs to do. She does seem to be reflecting on how things have happened back-to-back in her life and in a hurry and how she suddenly finds herself in another place. Hence she feels as though the pace of life was rapid and C is correct.

Notes

Notes

Notes

Notes

Notes

Notes

Notes

Essential Preparation for

UMAT

UNDERGRADUATE MEDICINE & HEALTH SCIENCES ADMISSION TEST

MULTIPLE CHOICE ANSWER SHEET

Use pencil when filling out this sheet

Fill in the circle correctly			
●			

If you make a mistake neatly cross it out and circle the correct response			
● (crossed out)	●	C	D

1	A	B	C	D	23	A	B	C	D
2	A	B	C	D	24	A	B	C	D
3	A	B	C	D	25	A	B	C	D
4	A	B	C	D	26	A	B	C	D
5	A	B	C	D	27	A	B	C	D
6	A	B	C	D	28	A	B	C	D
7	A	B	C	D	29	A	B	C	D
8	A	B	C	D	30	A	B	C	D
9	A	B	C	D	31	A	B	C	D
10	A	B	C	D	32	A	B	C	D
11	A	B	C	D	33	A	B	C	D
12	A	B	C	D	34	A	B	C	D
13	A	B	C	D	35	A	B	C	D
14	A	B	C	D	36	A	B	C	D
15	A	B	C	D	37	A	B	C	D
16	A	B	C	D	38	A	B	C	D
17	A	B	C	D	39	A	B	C	D
18	A	B	C	D	40	A	B	C	D
19	A	B	C	D	41	A	B	C	D
20	A	B	C	D	42	A	B	C	D
21	A	B	C	D	43	A	B	C	D
22	A	B	C	D	44	A	B	C	D

Essential Preparation for

UMAT

UNDERGRADUATE MEDICINE & HEALTH SCIENCES ADMISSION TEST

MULTIPLE CHOICE ANSWER SHEET

Use pencil when filling out this sheet

Fill in the circle correctly			
●	B	C	D

If you make a mistake neatly cross it out and circle the correct response			
	●	C	D

1	A	B	C	D	23	A	B	C	D
2	A	B	C	D	24	A	B	C	D
3	A	B	C	D	25	A	B	C	D
4	A	B	C	D	26	A	B	C	D
5	A	B	C	D	27	A	B	C	D
6	A	B	C	D	28	A	B	C	D
7	A	B	C	D	29	A	B	C	D
8	A	B	C	D	30	A	B	C	D
9	A	B	C	D	31	A	B	C	D
10	A	B	C	D	32	A	B	C	D
11	A	B	C	D	33	A	B	C	D
12	A	B	C	D	34	A	B	C	D
13	A	B	C	D	35	A	B	C	D
14	A	B	C	D	36	A	B	C	D
15	A	B	C	D	37	A	B	C	D
16	A	B	C	D	38	A	B	C	D
17	A	B	C	D	39	A	B	C	D
18	A	B	C	D	40	A	B	C	D
19	A	B	C	D	41	A	B	C	D
20	A	B	C	D	42	A	B	C	D
21	A	B	C	D	43	A	B	C	D
22	A	B	C	D	44	A	B	C	D

Essential Preparation for

UMAT

UNDERGRADUATE MEDICINE & HEALTH SCIENCES ADMISSION TEST

MULTIPLE CHOICE ANSWER SHEET

Use pencil when filling out this sheet

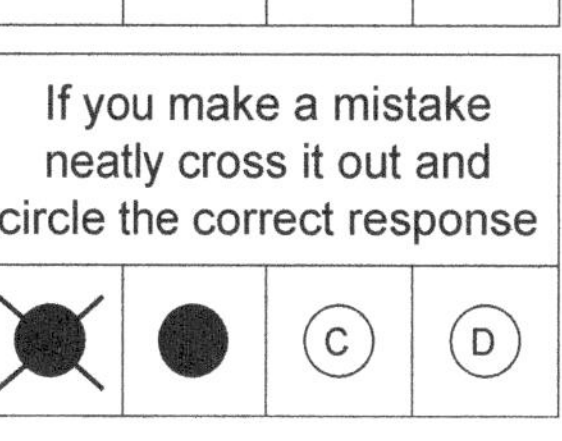

If you make a mistake neatly cross it out and circle the correct response

1	A	B	C	D
2	A	B	C	D
3	A	B	C	D
4	A	B	C	D
5	A	B	C	D
6	A	B	C	D
7	A	B	C	D
8	A	B	C	D
9	A	B	C	D
10	A	B	C	D
11	A	B	C	D
12	A	B	C	D
13	A	B	C	D
14	A	B	C	D
15	A	B	C	D
16	A	B	C	D
17	A	B	C	D
18	A	B	C	D
19	A	B	C	D
20	A	B	C	D
21	A	B	C	D
22	A	B	C	D
23	A	B	C	D
24	A	B	C	D
25	A	B	C	D
26	A	B	C	D
27	A	B	C	D
28	A	B	C	D
29	A	B	C	D
30	A	B	C	D
31	A	B	C	D
32	A	B	C	D
33	A	B	C	D
34	A	B	C	D
35	A	B	C	D
36	A	B	C	D
37	A	B	C	D
38	A	B	C	D
39	A	B	C	D
40	A	B	C	D
41	A	B	C	D
42	A	B	C	D
43	A	B	C	D
44	A	B	C	D